FROM MOURNING TO MORNING

Just as we will all die, so too we will all mourn the death of loved ones. Life prepares us for neither. Rabbi Schreiber's brilliantly insightful guide to mourning is an essential read for every human being who will someday grieve. **From Mourning to Morning** is an indispensable guided tour through the valley of the shadow of death – a place we will all visit. Rabbi Schreiber works in that valley every day, helping those in need of practical and spiritual advice – advice he generously shares in this invaluable book.

– Alan Dershowitz, Author of Abraham: The World's First (But Certainly Not Last) Jewish Lawyer

Rabbi Simeon Schreiber has authored a very important monograph about a very difficult subject. This clearly written guide will greatly help all who find themselves confronted by the imminence of death and its aftermath. It will also significantly benefit those who want to offer support and comfort at that time. Full of thoughtful sensitivity and deep Jewish wisdom, this work by a highly respected and beloved hospital chaplain offers practical guidance and advice gained from decades of experience dealing with these issues. This work is an indispensable aid for all who find themselves in this situation, as inevitably all of us will, learned and uninitiated alike.

– Rabbi Dr. Jacob J. Schacter, University Professor of Jewish History and Jewish Thought and Senior Scholar, Center for the Jewish Future, Yeshiva University

From Mourning to Morning makes a large and much-needed contribution to the Jewish community. It re-introduces to the modern reader many of the elements of Jewish traditional practice around death and mourning that have proven – over centuries – to provide great wisdom, insight and comfort to the bereaved. Today, when people are searching deeply for meaning in their lives and some shiva homes can more resemble cocktail parties than houses of mourning, this very clear "how to" manual for making a shiva call has never been more timely and needed. It is a useful and sensitive book for mourner and comforter alike. I hope every synagogue office and Rabbi's study everywhere is stocked with multiple copies for distribution to those in need of its guidance.

– Jacob Solomon, President and CEO, Greater Miami Jewish Federation

FROM Mourning
TO Morning

A COMPREHENSIVE GUIDE TO
MOURNING, GRIEVING, AND BEREAVEMENT

with *Special Emphasis on the Shiva Call*

RABBI SIMEON SCHREIBER

URIM PUBLICATIONS
Jerusalem • New York

KTAV PUBLISHING

From Mourning to Morning: A Comprehensive
Guide to Mourning, Grieving, and Bereavement,
with Special Emphasis on the Shiva Call

ISBN 978-965-524-261-4

Typeset by Ariel Walden for Urim Publications
Cover: Joelle Silverman Miller, By Design Communications

Printed in USA

Urim Publications
P.O. Box 52287
Jerusalem 9152102 Israel
www.UrimPublications.com

KTAV Publishing
527 Empire Blvd.
Brooklyn, NY 11225
orders@ktav.com
(718) 972-5449
www.ktav.com

Library of Congress Cataloging-in-Publication Data

Names: Schreiber, Simeon, author.
Title: From mourning to morning : a comprehensive guide
    to mourning, grieving, and bereavement : with special
    emphasis on the shiva call / Rabbi Simeon Schreiber.
Description: Brooklyn, New York : Urim Publications ;
    Jerusalem : Ktav Publishing, [2016]
Identifiers: LCCN 2016032578 | ISBN 9789655242614 (pbk. :
    alk. paper)
Subjects: LCSH: Jewish mourning customs. | Shivah (Jewish
    mourning custom) | Bereavement–Religious aspects–
    Judaism.
Classification: LCC BM712 .S37 2016 | DDC 296.4/45–dc23 LC
    record available at https://lccn.loc.gov/2016032578

With Sincere Gratitude and Appreciation

"Go out and seek the type of person to whom one should cling."
Rabbi Eliezer says, "One who possesses a good eye."
Rabbi Yehoshua says, "One who is a good friend."
Rabbi Yossi says, "One who is a good neighbor."
Rabbi Elazar says, "One who possesses a good heart."

Rabbi Yochanan ben Zakai says, "It is the words of Rabbi Elazar that I prefer, for one who possesses a good heart will incorporate all of the other qualities as well."

Excerpted from Pirkei Avot (Ethics of our Fathers),
Chapter 2, Mishna 14

In grateful appreciation to the good-hearted supporters whose confidence, trust and unselfish generosity made the publication of From Mourning to Morning *a reality.*

ANONYMOUS

ABRAHAM BORG

BELLA and STEPHEN BRENNER

ELTES Family

JUDY and FRED FARBMAN

SURI and BERT FRIED

ETELLA and HAIM MARCOVICI

SANDY and JERRY SELIGSOHN

TARGUM SHLISHI,
a Raquel and Aryeh Rubin Foundation

VISITING CHAPLAIN SERVICES

JONI and GEORGE WHITE

Contents

Contents

Preface

My father died more than fifteen years ago. My experience of sitting Shiva for him following his burial is embedded in my mind. There was one individual in particular whose visit to me was so memorable that it unwittingly provided the catalyst for me to become more involved and knowledgeable about the proper protocols and guidelines for paying a Shiva call. She sat in front of me and began recounting recollections of our families' relationship that spanned many decades. No detail was omitted throughout her lengthy recitation. She continued on with a year-by-year accounting — for a period of time which seemed to stretch unto eternity.

I remember turning to my brother, who was sitting next to me, and quietly remarking that we would probably die ourselves before she finished! When her visit finally concluded, I vowed to myself that I would never subject other mourners to such behavior and that perhaps someday I would write a book on what an effective Shiva call should be.

Now, years later, after writing my first book, *A Caring Presence – Bringing the Gift of Hope, Comfort and Courage,* and remembering the effort it took, I should have been discouraged from even thinking about a second attempt at authorship. Unless one is naturally gifted and able to express ideas, thoughts and emotions easily, writing a book — even on a topic with which one is familiar — is a stressful endeavor. So why did I choose to persevere and accept the challenge of a second book?

In my role as Rabbi and Senior Staff Chaplain at Mount Sinai Medical Center in Miami Beach, Florida, I am confronted almost daily by patients and their families seeking advice on how to deal with serious illness, life-threatening conditions, and often the possibility of imminent death. Dealing with these issues over the past decade, I believe I have acquired a certain insight, knowledge and understanding of how to properly respond to these difficult situations. Often I am asked to lecture to groups or serve as a panelist to offer my advice and perspective on these delicate and sensitive issues.

To be regarded as an expert by one's colleagues and peers is certainly a heady accolade. So when the suggestion was made that I convert my oral lectures into book form so that others might benefit from them, I remembered my earlier "promise" to myself to write on this topic, took a deep breath, consulted with my friends, my colleagues, my family and, with trust in God that He would guide my hand, agreed to do so.

But where to begin? What is the meaning of Shiva? What is its purpose for both the mourner and the visitor? What is proper behavior at the home of a mourner? When to visit? How long to stay? What should be spoken about? Are there topics to avoid? What if the mourner begins to cry? Is it permissible to make the mourner laugh? What questions should be asked and what avoided? What about sending flowers or food to the mourner? In short, what is proper conduct when visiting a mourner during the Shiva period?

Although many books have been written on the topic of *aveilut* (mourning), most deal with the halachic aspect, the many Jewish laws involved during this period. Few, if any, deal with the practical day-by-day, common sense practices that are so important to the fulfillment of this *mitzvah*. It is my hope that this book will provide answers to all the above questions, and many more. In addition to learning about the stages of mourning, we will discuss the concept of grief and its healing powers.

Through a scripted scenario, you will go as an observer on a virtual Shiva call. Afterwards, you will review the visit point by point in order to determine which of the visitors' actions were proper and beneficial, and which improper or detrimental. Finally, together we will examine the visit and develop guidelines for a proper, effective Shiva call.

I hope that, after reading this book, you will return to it from time to time as situations arise, so you become more comfortable with its guidelines. Remember, these precepts are not written in stone; they are merely suggestions and recommendations based upon years of personal experience. Feel free to adapt them to your own needs. I hope you will never have to make use of these instructions – but should the need arise, I pray you will become more comfortable in performing this *chessed shel emet* (true, enduring kindness) that has no reciprocal reward.

Introduction

I have some good news that I want to share with you. It's taken some time but, from all indications, it looks like we have finally conquered death!

Apparently, people don't die anymore. Just as the word "cancer" was rarely uttered years ago when that diagnosis was made because patients might become frightened and lose all hope of a possible cure, the word "death" is rarely used to describe the individual who has died. They "pass away" . . . they "depart" . . . we "lose" them . . . we "sustain a loss" . . . they "go to a better place" . . . they "are now with God" . . . and, as reported in the obituary column of one Los Angeles newspaper, they "didn't fulfill their life's expectancy potential." What wonderful news — if only it were true.

The concept of death is frightening to many people. Ever since the infamous 9/11 attack when terrorists struck the Twin Towers in New York City without warning, killing more than 3,000 people, the reality that death could occur suddenly, at any moment in our lives, reminded us that we human beings have no control over our destiny. Helplessness is a frightening feeling.

Yet, despite our fears, our vulnerability, our inability to predict the exact moment or circumstance of our death, we will — all of us — eventually die. As the famous Jewish philosopher, Woody Allen, remarked, "Life is a terminal illness."

It is written in the biblical book of Job (1:21), "The Lord giveth and the Lord taketh away," meaning that just as the Lord imbues every human body with a living soul, so too He removes that soul when the time comes. Coming to grips with the realization that the person we loved is no longer here, that we will no longer be able to feel his touch or hear her voice, is a painful experience. Jewish tradition understands this and, in its wisdom, provides a method to allow the distraught relatives to begin the necessary and cathartic process of grieving: the Shiva period.

Shiva is a Hebrew word that means the number seven. Used in the context of *aveilut*, or mourning, it refers to the seven-day period of mourning traditional Jews observe when a family member has died. It begins immediately after the burial has taken place. During the week of Shiva, family, friends and members of the community visit the mourners in the hope of bringing them some measure of comfort and consolation. This visit has become known as the Shiva call.

A uniquely Jewish experience, the Shiva call presents an extraordinary opportunity for both visitor and mourner to join one another in a truly meaningful spiritual and healing moment. The visitor is able to demonstrate a heartfelt sense of caring, love and empathy, while the mourner is able to use this opportunity as a cathartic release of feelings that need to be expressed rather than repressed. Together they share a kaleidoscope of emotions from sadness, loss and grief to comfort, solace and inner peace.

Prior to Death

Regrets: Could've . . . Should've . . . Would've . . .

It's a human trait always to seek reasons to rationalize or justify our behavior. If we can determine *why* we acted in a certain way, *why* we responded to a situation in a particular manner, we somehow feel better about ourselves and our abilities to make decisions and to behave responsibly. But when self-doubt creeps into our thought processes, we become uncomfortable. We become vulnerable to making critical errors in judgment and this diminishes us in our own eyes. This type of thinking, particularly in situations when our loved ones are terminally ill, is both useless and dangerous because it is self-defeating, and because it does not allow us to be fully present with them and comfort them.

The three most destructive terms that can be uttered by family members when trying to come to grips with the reality that their loved one is about to die are: could've, should've, and would've.

"If only we had gone to a fourth doctor for another opinion, the results *could've* been different . . . We *should've* listened to our friends who were in a similar situation and had experience with this condition . . . Had we only taken the advice of people who suggested alternative medicine, the outcome unquestionably *would've* been different."

Each of these responses engenders pangs of doubt, frustration and guilt in family members, does nothing to help them through this critical emotional phase, and prevents them from helping their dying loved one find comfort.

Why Has God Forsaken Me?

There are other emotions many people experience when grappling with the reality of imminent death. Conflicted feelings about God play a key role. Though many families face a fearful diagnosis with great faith, the emotional wear and tear of watching their loved one losing her or his battle for life can erode trust in Divine wisdom. If only we could understand why God, who is described as kind, compassionate and merciful, is acting toward our loved one and us in a way that is so hurtful. Some people assume they must have committed some wrong to deserve such punishment, and long to know what it was. We feel that if only we could comprehend His ways, perhaps our feelings of frustration, vulnerability – and yes, even anger toward Him – might be eased. But in the final analysis, we are finite and God is infinite; we are mortal and God is immortal. Only He knows what is best for our loved one and for us. Ultimately, we must have faith and trust that His actions, though not always understandable or desirable to us, are for the best; that, despite the outcome, God has not, and will not, abandon us.

Rather than dwell on self-destructive thoughts, guilt, and doubt, it is far better to concentrate on caring tenderly for our dying loved one who is still able to hear our voices and feel the warmth and love of our touch, though her or his life is ebbing.

The Pre-Mourning Period

For most people anxiously preparing for the death of a loved one, the process of mourning actually begins long before the death occurs. Try as they may to prepare themselves for the final and irrevocable reality that death will overtake life, it is almost impossible to do so. Nevertheless, there are ways to help the family ease their inescapable pain prior to and during the final moments of their loved one's life.

Human beings have been created with five sensory perceptions. It is believed that four of these — sight, smell, taste and touch — begin to diminish as one draws closer to death. The last one — hearing — is, according to most scientific evidence, the final one to be lost. Consequently, it provides a special opportunity for family and friends to express their final goodbyes in a very meaningful and heartfelt way.

Recognizing that the terminal person, despite outward physical appearances, can and does hear sounds and voices, allows for very intimate and personal closures. Even if a patient is in a medically comatose state and apparently oblivious to her or his surroundings, it is believed that hearing ability still remains intact.

It is during these final moments that loved ones should communicate their heartfelt feelings. Intimacy is important. One should touch the person, hold her hand, stroke his arm, kiss her forehead. Talk to him. Tell her how much you love her. Let him know that although he will be missed, you and everyone else will be okay.

Bless him with a safe journey to a place where he

will finally be at peace . . . comfortable and without pain, without worry . . . greeted by those who passed away before him and are waiting to welcome him into their warm and loving midst.

It is customary, in the presence of a terminally ill or dying person, to recite a confessional prayer known in Hebrew as *Viduy.* Although tradition suggests that the dying person himself recite this confession, when the person is unable to because of his physical condition, then someone else, a family member or close friend, may do so instead.

This prayer is not intended to seal the fate of the individual as irrevocable. Rather, it is meant to underscore God's role in this world and His ability to change the course of nature if He so desires.

My God and God of my ancestors, to You I turn at this moment of despair. I acknowledge that the gift of life is in Your hands. And though I earnestly pray for healing, I know that I am but mortal. Dear God, if in Your wisdom my life must soon come to an end, let me die, I pray, in peace. I confess that in my lifetime I have transgressed with sins and errors in judgment. But I also ask that You remember the good that I have done. May these acts of goodness, dear God, give meaning

21

to my life. May You, o Lord, forgive my transgressions so that in death I am granted atonement and purity. I pray, God of mercy, that as now I forgive all who have wronged me that they, in turn, grant me forgiveness as well.

Guardian of the bereaved, please protect my family and loved ones from excessive hurt and sorrow. Let them know that we will always be united, for our souls are surely entwined in eternal and mutual love. Shelter me, dear God, under Your protective wings as I place my soul into Your hands.

"The Lord gives and the Lord takes away;
may God's name be praised forever." Amen.

ה׳ נתן וה׳ לקח, יהי שם ה׳ מבורך מעתה ועד עולם
*Hashem natan v'Hashem lakach, yehi shem
Hashem m'vorach me'atah v'ad olahm.*

At the Moment of Death

The death of the elderly, or someone who has lived a full and meaningful life, is undoubtedly a sad occurrence. But the physical and emotional effect it engenders for the survivors is usually much less traumatic than the sudden and unexpected death of an infant, someone who was murdered, killed in an accident, or committed suicide.

Death from old age is part of the realistic cycle of life. By contrast, tragic deaths are unexpected and therefore usually create a dramatic behavioral response which manifests itself in many different ways. This response is called "shock syndrome." Shock is actually the body's way of protecting itself from the horrors of the moment.

Certain responses, such as screaming, rage, anger and hysteria are "action-based." They allow the individuals affected to respond by verbally and/or physically reacting. In some hospitals, usually adjacent to the emergency room where deaths often occur, there is a designated "screaming room." This room is constructed with padded walls that absorb sound and allow the individuals a solitary space where their emotions can be unleashed without embarrassment or disturbing others who may be in close proximity.

There is another type of common response which I would classify as "passive." No immediate actions are demonstrated. Generally, no outward rage or hysteria is displayed. Interestingly, this reaction does not necessarily begin to manifest itself at the moment the news of the death is announced. It is a response that is slow-growing but constant. It often begins at the first sign of the patient's illness, and continues throughout treatment. Even at the moment of death, and at times for months following the death, this emotion remains. It is the powerful and destructive state of denial. The inability to face reality, regardless of the circumstances, weakens an individual's capability to focus on positive solutions that will ultimately benefit the patient.

A brief scenario illustrating this state of denial:

A wife returns from a routine mammogram and reports to her husband her concern that the doctor has detected a suspicious growth.

"Don't worry; it's probably nothing," is his response.

Subsequently, a biopsy reveals a cancerous tumor. "It's probably a false positive, a mistake. You look healthy."

Two doctors recommend a radical mastectomy to be followed by chemotherapy and radiation. The husband responds, "Let's get a third opinion."

"I'm afraid I am going to die without treatment," the wife tells him.

"Let's pray; God will help."

After months of delaying and postponing treatment, the cancer metastasizes and the patient succumbs. Her death was not due to poor medical treatment, but to denial — a passive emotional response to shock syndrome. The husband and those who supported his denial, out of compassion, no doubt, will have to face how their decisions affected the situation.

Even when a patient and family members ostensibly accept a dreaded diagnosis and cooperate with treatment, denial can still furnish unrealistic hope that there will be a recovery against all odds. No matter how dire the patient's condition, the individual in denial will not be able to imagine that ultimate separation will occur. The idea of being parted forever is too frightening and the individual will mentally fight the notion, wholeheartedly believing that it will never happen. When the death of the loved one occurs, family members are truly caught off-guard and are unable to process the fact. Acceptance and grieving are delayed.

Whether the reaction was active or passive, at the moment of death there is little one can do immediately to soothe the mourners. Spoken words of consolation at this time are usually meaningless, mostly platitudes and refrains to calm the speaker more than they help the mourner.

Before the Shiva Begins

Judaism requires burial as soon as possible after death. This mandate creates a relatively short period of time between the death of an individual and the actual burial. During this time, as a sign of respect and reverence, the body of the deceased should not be left alone. In Orthodox Judaism, there are usually volunteers or relatives who remain with the body constantly. They are called *shomrim*, or watchmen. Throughout their period of watching, they may recite the chapters of *Tehillim*, the biblical book of 150 Psalms, to ensure that the body is blessed and protected by God. Depending upon the religious observance and desires of the family, the body of the deceased is cared for. Often it is ritually washed and cleansed and finally dressed in a white linen shroud prior to being placed in a simple pine coffin.

Death makes no distinction between rich and poor,

famous or unknown. The simple linen shrouds are a symbol of the equality of all mankind as every person passes from this world into another life. The pine boxes in which traditional Jewish families bury their loved ones are used so that the remains of the deceased return to the earth from which they originated as quickly as possible. This is in accordance with the biblical verse, "Man originates from dust and he shall return to the dust from which he came." (Genesis 3:14)

During this time, the relatives have not yet become official mourners and therefore are not bound by the specific laws pertaining to those who mourn. They are in limbo — a sort of holding pattern, a state between the memories of the deceased as he was in life and the acceptance of the new reality of his death. This in-between stage is called in Hebrew *aninut* and describes the unique time frame from a person's death until the actual burial. The individual mourner at this point in time is called an *onen*.

In accordance with traditional Jewish law, an *onen* is exempt (prohibited, in fact) from performing all of the positive *mitzvot* (commandments). As such, an *onen* does not pray, does not recite blessings of thankfulness to God, and a male *onen* does not put on *tefillin* (used in prayer). There are different opinions as to why the *onen* is exempt from performing any positive commandments. Judaism posits the following rule: "If a person is involved with performing a *mitzvah,* he is not required to start another *mitzvah* until the first act is completed." In years gone by, when an individual passed away, it was the remaining family members who took charge and became involved in all of the particulars and preparations of the burial process. Since they were involved in one *mitzvah,* the burial preparations, they were exempt from any other commandments.

In today's world, the family's participation in all of the preparations has become drastically diminished. Their role has been taken over by the burial society and the funeral parlor. The family's role has been reduced to notifying people about the time and place of the funeral service and placing an ad in the obituary columns of the local press. Consequently, the rationale for not performing a second *mitzvah* while involved with a first *mitzvah* is not as applicable anymore. Yet, an *onen* is still exempt from these *mitzvot,* and there are some excellent reasons why.

Rabbi Joseph B. Soloveitchik, who passed away in 1993, was considered one of the twentieth century's most brilliant and erudite Bible and Talmudic scholars. Rabbi Soloveitchik, who was also educated in philosophy, psychology, science and literature, served for

more than four decades at Yeshiva University's Rabbi
Isaac Elchanan Theological Seminary, the largest Orthodox rabbinical seminary in the USA. In discussing
the concept of *onen* and the prohibition of partaking
in formal rituals that might require the recitation of
a blessing, Rabbi Soloveitchik suggested an approach
that was different from the one mentioned above.

Rabbi Soloveitchik posited that the *onen* should not
perform any of the *mitzvot*, even if not involved in the
preparations and the details of the funeral. His reason-
ing was simple and psychologically sound. When the
death of a loved one occurs, sometimes unexpectedly,
sometimes tragically, a flood of emotions such as
shock, grief and denial overwhelm the mourner. But
there is often even a more powerful emotion that fills
the mourner – and that is anger. Anger at the event,
anger at oneself for not having been able to prevent it
from occurring, anger at the deceased for having died,
thereby leaving the mourner alone, frightened, unpro-
tected, vulnerable, scared. But most importantly, there
is often anger at God for having allowed the death to
occur and having caused so much sadness and grief.
Yes, anger at God Almighty, the kind, merciful and
compassionate God, who has forsaken us at this critical
time.

With this emotion stirring up such feelings of remorse and anger at God, how can one possibly perform even the simplest of acts or recite benedictions that begin with words of thanks and praise to this same God?

Therefore a note of caution to friends and family of the *onen* is in order: There is a great temptation to visit and offer words of comfort to the mourner in her or his home before the funeral. While laudable, I believe this assumption is both incorrect and improper. According to traditional Jewish law, only when one is an official mourner – after the burial – should words of consolation be offered. Jewish law reflects deep insight into human psychology. The mandate not to console the *onen* is based on the fact that expressions of solace to those who have yet to bury a loved one – "while the dead is still in his presence" – are actually counterproductive. Rather than console and comfort, the well-intentioned words often stir up feelings of annoyance, even anger. People need private time to reflect, to think, to plan. They need space to gather their thoughts and emotions. The *onen,* while needing the wordless, moral support of a loving family, at this time needs to be alone with his thoughts. How disrespectful and insensitive it is to our feelings when someone intrudes on our private world at this difficult time. Their words do not bring us comfort, but only add to our sadness. Their platitudes fall on deaf ears.

At the cemetery, however, as friends and family gather to pay their final respects and support the *onen*, a change begins to take place. Slowly, the knowledge of this new reality starts to take shape, and the *onen* begins to face the new truth that now must be accepted. The disbelief and shock begin to dissipate. The coffin is lowered into the ground. The sound of the earth thudding on the coffin shatters the silence and only then can one begin to accept the truth of the new reality and utter a blessing.

When this reality is affirmed and the *Kaddish* (mourner's prayer) – which speaks not of death but of God's omnipotence and omniscience – is recited, one is no longer an *onen*, unable to thank and praise God. The *onen* is transformed into an *aveil*, a mourner; one who, though unable to understand God's mysterious ways, nonetheless accepts them. Like the deceased, we too are God's creations and will receive His protection and love during this difficult period in our lives. The mourner is now ready to accept words of sympathy.

The Good Earth

"And God created man from the earth . . . and at the end of days . . . man shall be returned to the earth from which he was formed." (Genesis 3:19)

Recently, we have witnessed the popularization of an alternative to burial: cremation. Rather than inter the physical remains of the deceased directly into the earth, the remains are burned in a fiery furnace at extremely high temperature and are transformed into ashes. The ashes are either placed in a plain urn and buried at the cemetery in a special grave, or kept in a decorative urn as a memorial keepsake for the family. There is, unfortunately, an entire industry surrounding the cremation process. Jewelers create ornamental jewelry, such as lockets and bracelets, with compartments to hold the ashes of loved ones. Family members can wear these on their wrists or neck as a constant remembrance. If put under enormous and intense pressure, the ashes, which are actually carbon, can even be made into diamonds and placed into a ring for eternity.

One of the main reasons families choose cremation is that it is economical. The total cost of a standard funeral can be in excess of $15,000. Cremation may only cost in the neighborhood of $5,000. Death, like life, has its costs. Unfortunately, the value that is accorded to money sometimes far exceeds the value of dignified burial.

Judaism does not allow cremation, for human remains have sanctity and should not be marred or destroyed. Opposition to cremation is so strong that *Kaddish* is not recited for an individual who has chosen to have his or her body cremated. In addition, the seven-day Shiva period is not observed by his or her family. It is worth exploring the underlying reason for burial rather than cremation.

Judaism believes that the human being is comprised of two separate, but integrated, components: the physical body of flesh and bone, and the spiritual *neshamah* — the spirit and soul. The relationship of body and soul is symbiotic. They are not separate entities that have been synthesized, relinquishing their individual essence when joined to one another. Rather, they are one interdependent and interrelated whole, indivisible, each with its own holiness and sanctity, yet connected to and part of one complete new entity.

Picture, if you will, a holy ark made of precious and magnificent materials. Inside the ark have been placed the holy Torah scrolls. What would happen if the scrolls were suddenly removed to another place, thereby leaving the ark empty? Could one with a clean conscience dismantle the ark and use its components to build a piece of furniture? Wouldn't that be sacrilegious and irreverent? Wouldn't that be showing disdain and lack of respect for something that once housed holiness within its walls? So too is the relationship of the body and the soul of an individual. The death of an individual removes the holy soul from the body. The soul ascends heavenward to join the many souls of those previously departed. But the body — the holy receptacle that once housed the soul — remains here on earth to be returned to the soil from which it came. This holy receptacle that now is devoid of its holy soul still retains its essence of holiness, much the same as the holy ark still retains its holiness despite its emptiness. Can one, in good conscience, subject the holy body to disrespect and degradation?

The Funeral

Traditional funerals proceed in one of two ways, usually based upon the number of anticipated attendees. When large attendance is expected, a chapel ceremony is preferred. Family and friends gather at the funeral parlor, usually half an hour prior to the beginning of the formal services. (It is advisable to sign the register, so the mourners can later acknowledge those who attended.) They speak with one another, often expressing meaningful condolences to the mourners; but, unfortunately, more often chatting about irrelevant topics or expressing platitudes about the deceased to the mourners. This is meant as an attempt on the part of the visitors to console the mourners but usually it is an unconscious effort to make themselves more comfortable. The attendees are then invited into the chapel and seated to await the entrance of the mourners, who are usually escorted by the members of the clergy who will be officiating at the service.

Prior to the formal services, the mourners will be asked to perform the act of *kriah*, the tearing or the rending of their outer garments. Instead of tearing their garments as a tangible expression of their grief, many non-traditional Jews choose to pin a black ribbon onto their garments. Although both methods are commonplace and have become acceptable today, I believe the essence of mourning is compromised by using the ribbon.

When a loved one dies, whether naturally or tragically, the pain that is experienced by the mourners is indescribable. It is searing and intense, as if a piece of the mourner has been torn from the body. The tearing of one's outer garment is meant to symbolically express this emotional and irreparable tearing apart of one's own life. A loved one has been taken from our midst and the fabric of our lives will never be the same. The pinning of a black ribbon, although well-intentioned, can never be an effective substitute. It is perfectly permissible for mourners to wear clothing that is not valuable for this purpose.

When the deceased is a parent, the tear or the ribbon is always on the left side of the mourner's clothing,

above the mourner's heart. For all other immediate
family members, the tear or ribbon is placed on the
mourner's right. Prior to performing the tear or pinning the ribbon, the following blessing is recited both
in Hebrew and in English by the mourners, usually
with the help of the clergy.

> "Blessed are you, God, our God and King of the
> Universe, Who is the true Judge."
>
> ברוך אתה ה׳ אלוקינו מלך העולם דיין האמת
>
> *Bahrooch atah Adoshem Elokeinoo melech*
> *ha-olahm dayan ha-emet.*

Unlike the blessings forbidden to the *onen* that thank
God for the privilege of observing *mitzvot*, for food and
sustenance, or appreciation for His abundant kindness,
the blessing declaring God as the "true Judge" is one
of humility. I believe that the *onen* is permitted to say
this blessing because it does not conflict with his pain
and possible anger. It does not express gratitude, but
openly expresses our inability to say anything, our feeling of futility at a moment when there are no words to
express what we feel. So we essentially state, "We don't
understand this. We are speechless. Only *You* know
what is true and good for us."

The general concept expressed here is that only God
knows what is best for all of humanity. His judgment

is "true" in that it is perfectly accurate in its balance of justice and compassion. Though acceptance of this principle may be nearly impossible for the mourner to experience at this poignant moment, the practice plants the seed for recovery after the loss.

When ceremonies are held graveside – often a family preference – the religious requirements are much the same. The basic difference is that the graveside service will usually be abbreviated.

The chapel service traditionally begins with the recitation of a selection of readings from the Book of Psalms written by King David. The most popular psalm that is generally recited is Psalm 23, "The Lord is my shepherd." So that its content is understood by all, it may be read in both Hebrew and English. Often the attendees are asked to recite this psalm together with the reader. Other selections may also be read, such as Psalms 16, 25, 34, and 112, if the mourners request their recitation.

The officiating clergy will then deliver a eulogy in which the history, background, qualities and characteristics of the deceased are remembered and extolled. In some instances, other family members or close friends are encouraged to speak as well. It is their way of saying a final goodbye and psychologically serves as both a healthful and cathartic release of emotions and feelings.

Traditional ceremonies conclude with the chanting of the prayer *Keil maleh rachamim,* "Oh God . . . You Who are full of compassion." It asks that the soul of the deceased find rest under the sheltering wings of God and be protected as it journeys into the world of eternal rest and peace. The mourners follow the casket, which is carried or wheeled by selected pallbearers, as it makes its way to the hearse and then to the gravesite where it will be interred.

Additional prayers are recited at the cemetery. Attendees are often asked to help cover the casket by placing some soil into the grave. This deed is the final act of respect and remembrance, and psychologically aids in beginning the emotional closure that will be needed.

On some occasions, as a final gesture, a packet containing earth from the holy land of Israel is opened and the contents are added to the earth that is being shoveled onto the coffin that has been lowered into the ground. According to Maimonides, the earth of Israel offers atonement to the deceased. Since the deceased is not being buried in Israel, we bring Israel to him or her. (This custom only applies to those buried in the

Diaspora, since anyone buried in Israel receives atonement directly from the earth itself.)

Finally, the Mourners' *Kaddish* is recited. Interestingly, the *Kaddish* prayer says nothing about death or the deceased. It extols God as omnipotent and omniscient. It is intended to teach us that all is in God's hands, and that despite our loss and hurt we are able to proclaim, "The Lord gives and the Lord takes away; May His name be blessed forever."

At the conclusion of the burial services, the attendees are asked to face one another and form two parallel lines. The mourners exit the burial place by walking through the space that has been formed by the people facing one another in the parallel lines. As the mourners pass each individual, the following expression of comfort is recited by the attendees three times in succession,

"May God comfort you among the mourners of Zion and Jerusalem."

המקום ינחם אתכם בתוך שאר אבלי ציון וירושלים.
HaMakom yenachem et'chem b'toch sh'ar avaylay Tzion v'Yerushalayim.

When the mourners or those consoling them are of Sephardic descent, in addition to these customary words of consolation, the following statement is often recited,

"May your consolation be derived from God."
Min HaShamayim Tenuchamu.   מן השמיים תנוחמו

Even at this emotionally painful time, mourners often find this murmur of so many voices repeatedly offering consolation an uplifting and truly comforting experience.

Prior to leaving the cemetery, the mourners and all the attendees are required to wash their hands. This washing is not for sanitary purposes but, according to tradition, to cleanse the hands of any spiritual impurity present in the cemetery. Should one forget to wash, it can be done immediately upon returning to the place where the Shiva will be observed.

The Meal of Recovery and Condolence

It is customary *(only)* for the mourners to be served a small meal when they arrive at the Shiva home. This meal is served to them by friends and/or relatives. Traditionally, the meal – known in Hebrew as *seudat havra'ah,* literally a meal of recovery – should consist of food that is circular in shape. Bagels and hard-boiled eggs are the foods usually served because in a symbolic way they represent the emotional state of the mourners. Both foods have no "front" or "back;" they are without any opening, as is the new mourner whose mouth is closed, unable yet to speak about the loss that has just been sustained. Additionally, these round foods represent the circle and cycle of life.

Soon, the mourners take their places in the room where the Shiva will take place. According to tradition, they remove their leather shoes and replace them with canvas footwear or slippers. They sit on chairs or benches that are low to the floor, in accordance with ancient mourning practices.

When one stands tall and erect, one's appearance and stature are enhanced. There is a sense of dignity and importance conveyed by one's posture. It is noticed and one's presence is felt even without speaking. The mourner has been diminished by the death of a loved one. Who they are socially and what they possess materially are no longer relevant. They are merely human beings whose lives have been brought down as a consequence of their loved one's death. Sitting on chairs that are low to the floor, that almost touch the ground, demonstrates our recognition of our lowliness and vulnerability, and reminds us that we are mortals whose lives originate from the earth and will ultimately end in the earth as well.

Traditionally, the mirrors in the house of mourning are covered. Mirrors are reflective; they reproduce the outer image of the individual who is peering into them. A purpose of Shiva is to allow the mourners time to introspect, to reflect upon the lives of the deceased as well as their own inner selves. By covering the mirrors, we are saying that the true value and worth of individuals does not reside in their external reflection but in their internal essence.

The Shiva period has officially begun and the mourners begin their wait for the first visitors — family and friends who will attempt to offer consolation for the next seven days.

Grieving and Shiva

"The heart is the pillow for one's tears . . ."

Grieving is an emotional and physical response for individuals whose lives are changed when a loved one dies. Grieving allows the individual to release the pent-up feelings that death creates. Grieving is natural; grieving is healthful; grieving is psychologically sound. Grieving is not a sign of weakness; it is an indication of strength of character.

Why do we grieve? There is a natural three-step progression: attachment; loss; grief. When one is attached to something or someone and that object, situation or person is lost, the end result will be grief.

A toddler is attached to a teddy bear. A teenager is attached to her friends. A man is attached to his successful business. A husband and wife are attached to one another by marriage. A parent is attached to a child. When there is a loss, there will inevitably be grief.

Although many people are uncomfortable showing grief and view publicly expressed grief as inappropriate, they fail to understand the purpose and benefit of the grieving process. If you are old enough to remember the funeral of President John F. Kennedy, you will certainly recall the stoic poise and posture of Jacqueline Kennedy, standing ramrod straight as the funeral progressed, shedding not a tear, her little son John John holding her hand, standing at attention like a miniature solder, emotionless. To this family, a public display of grief would have been embarrassing. They believed that people of culture, character and breeding do not grieve publicly!

But, as with an infected boil filled with germs and pus, the cure and the healing process can only begin after the boil is punctured and the infected contents spill out. The initial pain is excruciating, but with time and healing, the pain begins to subside. So too, with death. The grieving process is painful; the deeper the attachment, the more intense the love, the deeper the pain upon loss.

Grieving is cathartic: it allows the emotions to pour forth uninhibited, and with the tears come the calmness and relief of stress that ultimately allow the individual to become whole again. Memories remain, but the pain eventually lessens.

There are many inaccuracies about the concept of grief.

Myths About Grieving

- It takes two months to get over your grief.
- Grief always declines over time in a steadily decreasing fashion.
- When grief is resolved, it never comes up again.
- Family members will always help grievers.
- Children grieve like adults.
- It is better to put painful things out of your mind.
- You should not think about your deceased loved one at the holidays because it will make you too sad.
- There is no reason to be angry at your deceased loved one.
- Children need to be protected from grief and death.
- You will have no relationship with your loved one after her or his death.
- It is better to tell bereaved people to "be brave" so they will not have to experience much pain.
- If you are a widow, you should grieve like other widows.

- Losing someone to sudden death is the same as losing someone to an anticipated death.
- It is not important for you to have social support during your grief.

What is most important to understand is that grief is not a "one size fits all" concept. Individuals grieve in their own particular manners, unique to them. No one can or should tell another person how to grieve or for how long a period. Equally important, and despite the good intentions of those paying a condolence call, no one can truly understand what the mourner is experiencing during this trying time. Understanding presupposes that one can be in the body and spirit of the mourner — an improbable and impossible condition.

The Shiva Call

Now that we have touched upon the possible responses and reactions that an individual might experience upon learning of the death of a loved one, it is time to visit that person who has begun "sitting Shiva." As noted previously, many people are uncomfortable performing this *mitzvah*. What to do, what not to do, what to say, what not to say, when to visit, how long to stay. Should food be brought or sent? What about flowers?

Together let's explore a typical Shiva visit. Keep
in mind that when you read the following scripted
scenario, you should focus on every action taken and
statement made. Had you been the individual sitting
Shiva, would you have found this visit meaningful and
comforting? Was something missing from the visit?
Were mistakes made? What would you have done
differently had you been the visitor? As an experiment,
take a blank sheet of paper and jot down both the pos-
itives and negatives of the visit. After that, we will review point by point the actions taken and the dialogue
spoken to see what lessons we can extrapolate from
this encounter.

Peter and Helene's Shiva Call

Peter and Helene moved into the neighborhood eighteen years ago, just two weeks after Jonathan and
Ruth. Although the couples are not best friends, they
certainly can be called good friends. Jonathan and
Ruth are traditional Jews, and Peter and Helene are
secular Jews not affiliated with any temple or religious
institution. Nonetheless, the two couples connect on
many different levels.

Upon hearing the news that Ruth's mother had
passed away, Peter immediately calls Helene. Even

though it means canceling tickets to a hit Broadway
show that they had looked forward to seeing for a long
time, both Peter and Helene agree that paying a Shiva
call promptly is far more important than a Broadway
show.

At 6:30 that evening, Peter and Helene walk up to
the front door of Jonathan and Ruth's house. They are
both nervous and uncomfortable: they don't know what
to expect, what to say, or how to act. They hope that
the flowers they sent to the house in memory of Ruth's
mother had arrived and would somehow provide some
cheer to the atmosphere. Peter rings the bell and waits.
When no one answers the bell after a second ring, he
pushes against the door. Surprisingly, it is open and
they enter. The house is quiet except for some voices
coming from the dining room. They notice that the
living room has many empty chairs set in a semi-circle,
so they walk in and sit down. Suddenly Ruth appears.
She looks slightly flustered. "I'll be with you in a moment," she apologizes, "I'm just finishing dinner."

A few minutes later, Ruth enters the living room and
sits down on a low chair in front of them.

"We're really sorry about your mother," begins Peter.

Ruth nods her head. "Thank you."

"But," continues Peter, "you're really lucky that she
passed away so quickly . . . no pain . . . no suffering . . ."

"Well . . . I suppose so," replies Ruth, her voice trailing off.

"Wasn't your mother around eighty-five years old?" asks Helene.

"Actually, she was only eighty-one when she passed away," answers Ruth.

"Well, you're fortunate she lived such a long life," Helene sighs. "My mother was fifty-eight when she died and she really suffered. She had breast cancer and nothing helped. Not the radiation, not the chemo; it was really a mess. She was in constant pain towards the end. I was only twenty-two years old back then; not married, living alone — it was really tough!"

Ruth looks at Helene with a faraway gaze in her eyes and merely nods her head.

"She's not being very responsive," Peter muses. *"I wonder if she's really glad we came."*

"This silence is killing me," thinks Helene. *"I've just got to say something to get her out of that mood."*

"You know, we had tickets tonight for that hit show we told you about," offers Helene, "but Peter and I felt so strongly about your loss that we just simply canceled."

"Really?" replies Ruth. "How thoughtful of you."

"Did she say that sarcastically?" thinks Helene. *"Or did she really mean it?"*

"I've got an idea," Peter chimes in. "When all this is over, we should try to resume our weekly tennis get-to-gethers. You and Helene really make a great doubles team! It'll be good for you to get out, and you won't have to think about your mother's death so much."

"Well," replies Ruth softly, "when I'm ready, we'll see."

Feeling a little uncomfortable about how the conversation is progressing, Peter looks around the room. A couple with two young children, a girl and a boy, had just arrived. The girl appears to be around four years old and the boy, presumably her brother, is no more than a year old.

Peter whispers to Helene that it seems kind of strange to bring children, particularly that age, to the house of a mourner. Almost immediately, the four year old begins running around the room uncontrollably, bumping into furniture, while the one-year-old begins crying and howling loudly. After unsuccessfully attempting to quiet their children, the embarrassed parents quickly gather them up and leave — unfortunately, without having the opportunity to properly express their respects and wishes of consolation.

To lighten the mood, Peter and Helene fill Ruth in on all the latest neighborhood gossip. Helene mentions a great clothing sale, which would still be going on after

Ruth's Shiva period has passed. Peter remarks how awful business has become, especially due to the stock market's decline. Ruth's responses are short and seemingly without feeling.

"I wonder if she's really been affected by her mother's death," thinks Peter. *"She's so quiet and emotionless."*

Another visitor arrives, and a few moments later, yet another. Apparently the two visitors have not seen each other in a while and they engage in a lively, nostalgic conversation. The undertone of their banter fills the air. Every now and then, Ruth stares vacantly in their direction.

After twenty-five minutes of chatter, Peter and Helene notice that many other people have entered the room. They signal to each other that it is time to go.

"I hope the flowers we sent in your mom's memory will cheer you up somewhat," says Peter.

"And," continues Helene, "we've asked a kosher caterer to send over a large platter of cold cuts, salads – with all the trimmings! – so that you and your company will have something to eat."

"That was really very kind of you," Ruth responds. "Thank you so much for being so thoughtful."

Peter stands up, while Helene leans over and kisses Ruth on the cheek.

"Well, goodbye . . . we're really sorry," says Helene.

"We hope you have no more sorrows in your life for a long time. We'll be talking to you real soon."

"Thank you for visiting me," Ruth answers.

As Peter and Helene walk towards the front door, they notice a silver tray with a few dollar bills stacked on it. Above it is a sign with some Hebrew letters that they cannot read.

"That's strange," Peter quips. "It looks like there's an admission charge for visiting!"

Helene chuckles and soon they are outside and on their way home.

"Whew," said Peter. "We did it! And you know," he continues, "it wasn't as scary as I thought it would be!"

A Closer Look at Peter and Helene's Shiva Visit

You've observed Peter and Helene's Shiva visit. Did you jot down the things that looked just fine — things that perhaps you yourself would have done? How many were there?

What about the actions that Peter or Helene took that you felt were wrong or improper? How many of these were you able to identify? Perhaps you felt that the entire visit was flawed, that it was completely improper and not a very good example of what a Shiva call is all about. Or perhaps you felt that it was excellent, and that you would have acted just as Peter and Helene did in every aspect. Let's review the entire visit slowly, point by point, to see what lessons can be learned.

Before we begin, there is one critical point that has

to be made: anyone involved in the noble *mitzvah* of a Shiva call is always well intentioned. At no time should we ever view a visitor's motivations or behavior in any other way. Though sometimes faulty, the efforts always are sincere expressions of concern for the benefit of the mourner. My ultimate goal is to make certain that visitors maximize their important role as comforters and messengers of *chessed* (kindness).

Shiva Visit Guidelines

Now let's analyze the scripted scenario of Peter and Helene's visit one point at a time.

Peter and Helene moved into the neighborhood eighteen years ago, just two weeks after Jonathan and Ruth. Although the couples are not best friends, they certainly can be called good friends. Jonathan and Ruth are traditional Jews, and Peter and Helene are secular Jews not affiliated with any temple or religious institution. Nonetheless, the two couples connect on many different levels.

The first paragraph is simply factual. It establishes the relationship between the two couples. Because their different religious orientations are stressed, it sets the stage for a Shiva visit that, though well intentioned, may be uncomfortable — but instructive.

Upon hearing the news that Ruth's mother had passed away, Peter immediately calls Helene. Even though it means canceling tickets to a hit Broadway show that they had looked forward to seeing for so long, both Peter and Helene agree that paying a Shiva call promptly is far more important than a Broadway show.

Canceling their tickets was certainly a heartfelt and meaningful gesture by Peter and Helene and a strong indication of their friendship for Ruth and Jonathan. Had they been more knowledgeable about Shiva visiting protocols, however, they would have known that an immediate visit by non-family members is not only unnecessary but often discouraged, and even considered inappropriate, during the first few days of mourning. Because the Shiva period consists of seven days, Peter and Helene could have kept their theater tickets and enjoyed the show. Their Shiva visit could have taken place at any other time during the week.

At 6:30 that evening, Peter and Helene walk up to the front door of Jonathan and Ruth's house.

Was there a reason why Peter and Helene chose to visit at that specific time? Was it that it was the most convenient time for them, or had they inquired and determined that it was the most convenient time for Ruth?

In recent years it has become standard procedure to include the visiting time schedules in all communications regarding the Shiva period. If Peter and Helene had not been informed, a phone call to Jonathan would have told them when meals would be served so they could better time their visit. However, since they did not inquire, Peter and Helene did not know that it was dinner time, certainly not the best time for a visit.

GUIDELINE 1: Remember that a Shiva call is not about you! It is about the mourner and his/her needs.

They are both nervous and uncomfortable: they don't know what to expect, what to say, or how to act. They hope that the flowers they sent to the house in memory of Ruth's mother had arrived and would somehow provide some cheer to the atmosphere.

The sending of flowers to mourners, though a well-intentioned gesture, is not a Jewish custom. The purpose of the Shiva period is not to cheer up the mourners with gifts or conversations that take their minds off their loss. On the contrary, its purpose is to allow the mourners the opportunity to talk, reminisce, laugh and cry about someone whom they will no longer be able to speak with, touch or feel. Actions and gestures that are festive, such as sending flowers, serving alcoholic drinks, and preparing lavish food displays disturbs the solemnity of the visit and negates the true purpose and essence of this holy and sacred time.

GUIDELINE 2: Do not send flowers or any other festive items that detract from the solemnity of the Shiva period.

Peter rings the bell and waits. When no one answers the bell after a second ring, he pushes against the door. Surprisingly, it is open and they enter.

The Shiva call is both a personal and community responsibility. As such, permission to visit is not required; the door to the Shiva home always remains open, symbolically welcoming all who want to enter to express condolences and words of consolation. Ringing the doorbell suggests that one is requesting permission from those inside to enter, which is contrary to the purpose of the visit.

**GUIDELINE 3: Do not ring the doorbell. It is
expected that you will enter without ringing
the bell.**

---

*The house is quiet except for some voices coming
from the dining room. They notice that the living
room has many empty chairs set in a semi-circle, so
they walk in and sit down. Suddenly Ruth appears. She
looks slightly flustered. "I'll be with you in a moment,"
she apologizes. "I'm just finishing dinner."*

As noted previously, Peter and Helene were unaware
of the visiting time schedule that had been determined
by Ruth and therefore assumed that any time would
be appropriate. Mourners need some private time to
reflect, to reminisce, and to share memories with their
immediate family members. What better time to do
this than meal times, when one is alone with only the
people who are closest and most understanding. If a
schedule of meal times has not been made available,
and there is no one to contact with questions, common
sense should dictate times to avoid.

Often the family of the mourners will set specific
times for meals or prayer services and post these
times on the door of the home. If the sign on the door

stipulates no calls after a certain hour, be sure to heed the request and make sure you leave before that time. Also, do not enter the house after that time; come back at a time that is convenient for the mourner. Adherence to these time schedules will make both the mourner and the visitor more comfortable and allow for the maximum value from the time spent visiting.

GUIDELINE 4: Determine the time schedule for meals and prayer services.

A few minutes later, Ruth enters the living room and sits down on a low chair in front of them.

"We're really sorry about your mother," begins Peter.

Ruth nods her head. "Thank you."

Not knowing how to start or what to say, Peter began the conversation. Although his sentiments were truly sincere and heartfelt, and elicited a "thank you" response from Ruth, Jewish tradition requires that any opening statement be initiated by the mourner, not the visitor. This allows the mourner to direct the tone and subject of the conversation and how it should proceed.

Although in this instance, Peter's opening remark

was innocuous and sincere, there are often times when
visitors will begin their conversation with unintention-
ally foolish remarks, not knowing how the mourner
is feeling. ("It must have been a long day, but you're
looking good.")

**GUIDELINE 5: Allow the mourner to initiate the
conversation.**

---

*"But," continues Peter, "you're really lucky that
she passed away so quickly . . . no pain . . . no
suffering . . ."*

*"Well . . . I suppose so," replies Ruth, her voice
trailing off.*

Without giving Ruth the opportunity to respond in a
meaningful way or to redirect the questioning, Peter
continues with a trite remark that is so common. Does
Peter really believe that Ruth is feeling "so lucky" to
have lost her mother? The loss of a parent under any
circumstance is a painful experience. An unfillable
void has been created. Ruth will never be able to speak
to or touch her mother again — how can she possibly
feel "lucky" in any way at this moment? Her response
reflects those sentiments.

GUIDELINE 6: Don't make statements that can be construed as untrue or hurtful.

¶ "Wasn't your mother around eighty-five years old?" asks Helene.

"Actually, she was only eighty-one when she passed away," answers Ruth.

"Well, you're fortunate she lived such a long life," Helene sighs. "My mother was fifty-eight when she died and she really suffered. She had breast cancer and nothing helped. Not the radiation, not the chemo; it was really a mess. She was in constant pain towards the end. I was only twenty-two years old back then; not married, living alone — it was really tough!"

Ruth looks at Helene with a faraway gaze in her eyes and merely nods her head.

Helene's intention was to make Ruth feel fortunate and appreciative, that in the final analysis her mother had lived a long and fruitful life. However, comparing her own mother's short life filled with illness, pain and suffering, is without doubt inappropriate and insensitive — though this is a method used by so many well-meaning people. It is little consolation to the mourner that your loss was comparable or even more painful. No one can truly understand the depth of feeling, the sense of sadness, the loss and emptiness that another person is suffering. Comparisons are not only meaningless but hurtful as well.

This pain is reflected in Ruth's faraway gaze.

GUIDELINE 7: Do not make comparisons or references to your personal losses.

"She's not being very responsive," Peter muses. "I wonder if she's really glad we came."

"This silence is killing me," thinks Helene. "I've just got to say something to get her out of that mood."

There are times when silence is more meaningful than sound and is more appreciated. What is important to the mourner is not necessarily the words that are spoken, but the mere caring presence of the visitor. The mourner is experiencing a jumble of emotions, particularly during the first days of the Shiva period. Memories of the past mingle with lost hopes for the future; yesterday's joys merge with the sadness of tomorrow. It is not easy to focus and concentrate on all that is going on. At such times, quiet reflection helps the mourner.

Rather than analyze Ruth's lack of responsiveness, Peter and Helene should recognize the state of mind she is experiencing. Their role is not necessarily to speak, but rather, just to be with her at this difficult transitional time in her life.

GUIDELINE 8: Just "be there" for the mourner; don't be afraid of silences.

"You know, we had tickets tonight for that hit show we told you about," offers Helene, *"but Peter and I felt so strongly about your loss that we just simply canceled." "Really?" replies Ruth. "How thoughtful of you."*

"Did she say that sarcastically?" Helene thinks. "Or did she really mean it?"

"I've got an idea," Peter chimes in. "When all this is over we should try to resume our weekly tennis get-togethers. You and Helene really make a great doubles team! It'll be good for you to get out, and you won't have to think about your mother's death so much."

"Well," replies Ruth softly, "when I'm ready, we'll see."

Feelings of discomfort often bring out the worst in people. Not knowing what to say, how to act, which topics to address and which to avoid – especially in a new situation – creates a level of unease that is difficult to manage. To counteract this feeling, individuals will generally resort to talking about topics about which they are knowledgeable and comfortable. However, a house of mourning is not the place where this tactic should be utilized.

The purpose of the Shiva visit is to allow the mourners an opportunity to open up, to grieve, to express the feelings and emotions they are experiencing. This is psychologically necessary and a healthful and cathartic release of pent-up emotions. While not every mourner will want to talk about and relive memories of the deceased during the entire Shiva, visitors may want to ask a question or two that will help the mourner release those memories and reflect. It is always appropriate to say, "Tell us a little about your mother." It is the mourner's prerogative to respond in a manner that suits his or her mood at that moment.

GUIDELINE 9: Focus on conversations that are meaningful, not mundane, and try to elicit meaningful responses from the mourner.

Feeling a little uncomfortable about how the conversation is progressing, Peter looks around the room. A couple with two young children, a girl and a boy, had just arrived. The girl appears to be around four years old and the boy, presumably her brother, is no more than a year old.

Peter whispers to Helene that it seems kind of strange to bring children, particularly that age, to the house of a mourner. Almost immediately, the four year old begins running around the room uncontrollably, bumping into furniture, while the one-year-old begins crying and howling loudly. After unsuccessfully attempting to quiet their children, the embarrassed parents quickly gather them up and leave — unfortunately, without having the opportunity to properly express their respects and wishes of consolation.

Should children be brought to a Shiva call? That depends on the age and temperament of the child. Children as young as four serve no purpose at a Shiva visit and, as seen in the scenario, can be disruptive as well. Bringing a baby to "cheer up" the mourners is also inappropriate. If the parents cannot find a babysitter for young children, it would be better for only one parent at a time to pay the Shiva call.

In deciding whether or not to bring older children, consider: Are they able to understand that visitors are there to console someone whose relative has just died?

Can they understand the concept of death? Would it frighten them? Have their parents explained to them in advance how to behave?

If their behavior will be disruptive and negatively impact the solemnity of the visit, then children should not be brought along on a Shiva call. Obviously, if the children are related to those sitting Shiva, there should certainly be some flexibility. We must always remember that the Shiva visit is not about the visitor. The visitor's obligation is always secondary to what is important and consoling to the mourner.

GUIDELINE 10: Children should not visit if their conduct will be disruptive.

To lighten the mood, Peter and Helene fill Ruth in on all the latest neighborhood gossip. Helene mentions a great clothing sale, which would still be going on after Ruth's Shiva period has passed. Peter remarks how awful business has become, especially due to the stock market's decline. Ruth's responses are short and seemingly without feeling.

"I wonder if she's really been affected by her mother's death," thinks Peter. "She's so quiet and emotionless."

Just as the mention of a postponed activity or the proposal to continue playing tennis together are inappropriate conversations, so too are other topics such as clothing sales and stock market fluctuations. Some visitors even try to tell a joke to liven up the atmosphere. The reason visitors gravitate to these topics is because of a basic misconception about the true purpose and significance of the Shiva visit: Shiva is *not* intended to make the mourner feel better by avoiding any discussion of the deceased. Though it is a gathering of people, it is *not* a party. Quite the contrary, the reason for the Shiva call is to allow the mourner the opportunity to discuss, reminisce, cry, and even to laugh when remembering her or his loved one. It is only through this cathartic psychological cleansing that the healing process can begin, and ultimately allow the mourner to begin to live her or his new reality of a life without the loved one. Peter mistakenly thinks that the reason for Ruth's short and emotionless responses is that she is not affected by her mother's death. In truth, she is not responding because the topics Peter and Helene are raising are inappropriate.

GUIDELINE 11: Always keep in mind the true purpose of the Shiva visit: to help the mourner begin to heal in his or her own way.

Another visitor arrives, and a few moments later, yet another. Apparently the two have not seen each other in a while and they engage in a lively, nostalgic conversation. The undertone of their banter fills the air. Every now and then, Ruth stares vacantly in their direction.

GUIDELINE 12: Do not chat with other visitors. It is disrespectful and distracting to the mourner. If you must speak with someone other than the mourner, do so in another room.

After twenty-five minutes of chatter, Peter and Helene notice that many other people have entered the room. They signal to each other that it is time to go.

As noted above, a Shiva call is not a social visit. Unless the mourner indicates otherwise, by a verbal request or some other gesture, a Shiva visit should last no more than ten to fifteen minutes. The visitor should recognize that there may be other friends and relatives who are waiting to pay their respects. Moreover, mourners tire easily after a day of constant and repetitive conversation. Remember, it is not the length of the visit that is important; it is the sincerity of the visitor and the content of the conversation.

GUIDELINE 13: Do not visit for more than fifteen minutes, unless the mourner asks you to stay longer.

¶ *"I hope the flowers we sent in your mom's memory will cheer you up somewhat," says Peter.*

"And," continues Helene, "we've asked a kosher caterer to send over a large platter of cold cuts, salads – with all the trimmings! – so that you and your company will have something to eat."

"That was really very kind of you," Ruth responds. "Thank you so much for being so thoughtful."

Knowing that Peter and Helene are uninformed in Shiva protocol, Ruth politely thanks them for their thoughtfulness. There is universal agreement that sending flowers to a Shiva is inappropriate since flowers usually denote celebration and festive occasions, quite the opposite of the mood in the mourner's home. However, there are mixed opinions concerning the sending of lavish food platters not intended for consumption by the mourners, but for the many visitors who arrive during the day and evening. As previously noted, Shiva visiting is not a social gathering with small talk, alcohol and food consumption. The solemnity of the purpose is destroyed when the sanctity of the visit is distorted. To avoid the connotation of a party, food platters should be kept at a minimum so that the Shiva call retains its dignity.

GUIDELINE 14: Avoid sending elaborate food platters for visiting non-mourners.

¶ . . ."*so that you . . . will have something to eat.*"

Although there are differing opinions regarding sending food platters intended for visitors, there is no question about the need to make certain that the mourners and their immediate family members are well fed throughout the seven day mourning period.

Members of the synagogue, friends and relatives of the mourner often will take the responsibility of providing all the meals for the mourners. This is truly an act of kindness; one that will always be remembered and genuinely appreciated.

Of course, all food that is provided should be strictly kosher with the kosher seal of approval from a recognized rabbinical kashrut agency.

GUIDELINE 15: If possible, provide meals for the mourners and immediate family members.

¶ *Peter stands up, while Helene leans over and kisses Ruth on the cheek.*

"Well, goodbye . . . we're really sorry," says Helene. "We hope you have no more sorrows in your life for a long time. We'll be talking to you real soon."

"Thank you for visiting me," Ruth answers.

Before leaving the home of the mourners it is customary to recite words of consolation in Hebrew and/or English. When the mourners or those consoling them are of Sephardic descent, the following statement is often recited,

"May your consolation be derived from God."

Min HaShamayim Tenuchamu.   מן השמיים תנוחמו

In all other situations, it is customary to recite the following Talmudic passage,

"May God comfort you amongst the mourners of Zion and Jerusalem."

המקום ינחם אתכם בתוך שאר אבלי ציון וירושלים.

HaMakom yenachem et'chem b'toch sh'ar avaylay Tzion v'Yerushalayim.

Why is this specific wording used; what is the intent of this ancient expression? The Hebrew word for God's name used in this context is *HaMakom* (The Place), for it tells us that during this sad time in the lives of the mourners that *HaMakom*, the ever-present God, still resides among them in "this place;" that He will always be with them in their sorrow and will eventually allow them to face their new reality with renewed hope for the future.

But why do we also refer to those who mourn the destruction of Zion and Jerusalem, and ask God to console the mourners "among them"? What possible connection can our personal loss have with those who mourn the fall of Jerusalem and the destruction of the Holy Temple thousands of years ago?

I believe the answer lies not in the context of the loss, but in the vision, the promise and the hope for the future. For just as in our prayers (recited three times daily) we invoke God's mercy and compassion and ask that He restore to us "speedily in our days" the holiness of His presence in Jerusalem, so too we yearn for the restoration of the holy souls of our loved ones who have departed from us. Jewish tradition maintains that along with the restoration of the city and the Temple, the souls of the deceased will return to this world. Yes, today we mourn their loss, but our consolation is in the knowledge of their ultimate renewed life and a better tomorrow.

GUIDELINE 16: Upon taking leave of the mourners, face them and recite the traditional blessing: May God comfort you amongst the mourners of Zion and Jerusalem.

המקום ינחם אתכם בתוך שאר אבלי ציון וירושלים.

Hamakom yenachem et'chem b'toch sh'ar avaylay Tzion v'Yerushalayim.

The Sephardic custom is to recite: May your consolation be derived from God.

מן השמים תנחמו.

Min HaShamayim Tenuchamu.

As Peter and Helene walk towards the front door, they notice a silver tray with coins and a few dollar bills stacked on it. Above it is a sign with some Hebrew letters that they cannot read.

"That's strange," Peter quips. "It looks like there's an admission charge for visiting!"

As Peter and Helene exit Ruth's home, they come upon a strange sight, something they have never encountered previously — a tray stacked with coins and dollar bills. Peter mistakenly assumes that there may be an "admission charge" as part of the Shiva protocol, but that is not the case.

In Jewish tradition, giving charity to support those who are poor and less fortunate is one of the three pillars on which Judaism is founded. The giving of *tzedakah* – i.e., sharing our possessions, caring for others in a meaningful and material way – is not only an act of kindness or compassion. It expresses the philosophy that whatever we possess is truly not ours. It has been given to us by God so that we can share what is His with those who are His creations. In the house of a mourner, charity boxes or trays are placed to allow visitors the opportunity to participate in the *mitzvah* of *tzedakah*. The giving of charity at the Shiva is considered a merit for the deceased. The donations collected are often for organizations that provide medical care which may have been of service during the illness of the deceased. Sometimes funds are also collected for a particular charity that was close to the heart of the deceased. It is a great comfort to the family to turn over these funds in the name of the deceased at the end of the Shiva.

GUIDELINE 17: One should give charity as an act of kindness and compassion at the Shiva.

The Do's and Don'ts
of a Proper Shiva Call

Now that we have analyzed the Shiva visit by Peter and Helene, it seems apparent that almost all of what they said and did, though well-intentioned, could have been improved upon. Let's quickly review what a Shiva visit is, and what it is not.

A Shiva Call Is:

- Often a highly emotional time for the mourners and the visitors
- Intended to allow the mourners an opportunity to mourn, grieve, remember, laugh and share. They should feel a sense of caring from friends, family and community.
- Often a time for tears, touching and for silence
- Always a time to listen

A Shiva Call Is Not:
- Always comfortable or pleasant for the mourners and visitors
- An excessively lengthy visit
- An occasion for socializing with friends and family
- A time for loud conversation, idle talk, gossip or frivolity
- An opportunity to discuss business, weather, fashion, sports or the stock market
- A time for reminiscing about the visitor's own personal losses

Let us review the essential list of Guidelines that we developed:

GUIDELINE 1: Remember that a Shiva call is not about you! It is about the mourner and his/her needs.

GUIDELINE 2: Do not send flowers or any other festive items that detract from the solemnity of the Shiva period.

GUIDELINE 3: Do not ring the doorbell; knock gently and walk in.

GUIDELINE 4: Determine the time schedule for meals and prayer services.

GUIDELINE 5: Allow the mourner to initiate conversation.

GUIDELINE 6: Don't make statements that can be construed as untrue or hurtful.

GUIDELINE 7: Do not make comparisons or references to your personal losses.

GUIDELINE 8: Just "be there" for the mourner; don't be afraid of silences.

GUIDELINE 9: Focus on conversations that are meaningful, not mundane, and try to elicit meaningful responses from the mourner.

GUIDELINE 10: Children should not visit if their conduct will be disruptive.

GUIDELINE 11: Always keep in mind the true purpose of the Shiva visit: to help the mourner begin to heal in his or her own way.

GUIDELINE 12: Do not chat with other visitors.

GUIDELINE 13: Do not visit for more than fifteen
minutes, unless the mourner asks you to stay longer.

GUIDELINE 14: Avoid sending elaborate food
platters for visiting non-mourners.

GUIDELINE 15: If possible, provide meals for the
mourners and immediate family members.

GUIDELINE 16: Upon taking leave of the mourners,
face them and recite the traditional blessing:
"May God comfort you amongst the mourners of
Zion and Jerusalem."

המקום ינחם אתכם בתוך שאר אבלי ציון וירושלים.

*HaMakom yenachem et'chem b'toch sh'ar avaylay
Tzion v'Yerushalayim.*

The Sephardic custom, again, is to recite:
"May your consolation be derived from God."

Min HaShamayim Tenuchamu.   מן השמיים תנוחמו.

GUIDELINE 17: One should give charity as an act of
kindness and compassion at the Shiva.

Suggested Topics of Conversation at a Shiva Call

Meaningful topics elicit meaningful responses. If the issues Peter and Helene chose to speak about were unsuitable, what topics would have been better for discussion? What general or specific questions or comments might be asked to elicit meaningful responses from the mourners?

Since the main purpose of a Shiva call is to *allow the mourners an opportunity to talk about their loss*, questions or statements from the visitors should be framed in a way that allows the mourners to respond easily and meaningfully. To encourage such conversation, it is appropriate, where applicable, to ask questions such as:

I really didn't know your _____. Could you tell me what he/she was like?

What a perfect opening you've provided for the mourner to reflect upon the life of the deceased. A wellspring of information will pour forth: aspects of their lives — friendships shared . . . holidays enjoyed . . . charitable institutions supported — as well as little-known facts only now being revealed. Though the loved one has passed away, sharing the memories and good deeds will enable the mourner to keep the individual alive during this difficult transitional time in their lives.

(Presuming the deceased was a parent:)
How did your parents meet?

Another perfect opening and provocative question! People's lives are comprised of accomplishments and memories. Despite the normal ups and downs that many marriages experience, on the whole, marriages are happy, enjoyable, loving and successful. If there is a romantic aspect to the time that the parents first met, it will never be forgotten. Recounting that experience will certainly bring a smile to the mourner, despite the sadness that also will be present. So let them talk, re-live, and enjoy — and bask in the experiences and the beautiful memories of the romantic past.

How long were they married?

Although most people will answer this question with a simple numerical response given in length of years, one can never be certain what the reply will be. The most beautiful, touching and meaningful answer I've ever received to this question was, "Not long enough." What a magnificent sentiment to express.

What will you miss most about____?

This question will probably elicit both the quickest
and the most poignant response of all. "I will never be
able to speak to him again . . . I will never be able to
hear the reassuring tone of her voice . . . I will never be
able to have our daily 'cup of coffee' conversations . . . I
will never hear 'good night, I love you' again . . ."

There are many interactions and activities in one's
lifetime that fill the days of individuals and families.
Weekends spent together, the excitement of sport-
ing events, family outings, summer trips, holiday
feasts — all leave indelible memories. But the simple
sound of a loved one's voice — its tone, its inflection,
its pitch — remains with the mourner more than any
other memory. Many people choose to leave the voice
of the deceased individual on the outgoing voice mail
message so that each time the telephone number is
dialed, the voice of their loved one will be heard. Each
person's voice is special and unique; more than any
other characteristic, it unmistakably identifies and describes the individual. Being unable to hear that voice
will remain painful for the mourner until the healing
process eventually begins to take effect. My personal
belief is that, though this is a common practice, it is
actually detrimental because, as difficult as it may be,

it does not allow the mourners the ability to come to grips with their unfortunate new reality.

Was _____'s passing expected? Was someone with _____ when he/she passed away?

Consideration should be given before asking this "double-edged" question. On the one hand, if the death was expected, should one automatically assume the family remained with the dying individual until death occurred? Perhaps not. Not everyone has the emotional stamina to witness a loved one's death. In some cases, the patient may have requested to be alone. On the other hand, if the family was with the patient, they may take great comfort in that fact. So be careful with this question.

I am sure this must be very painful, how are you doing?

As noted throughout, the Shiva call is intended to allow the mourners an opportunity to mourn their loss. By reliving memories, hearing previously unknown stories revealed, and meeting individuals from their past, the pain of the mourner's loss begins to surface. No one can truly understand the depth of the mourner's pain. People are individuals, and our feelings, emotions, and sensitivities are uniquely ours alone. To tell someone that you "understand" what they are experiencing because you suffered a similar loss is not only false but insensitive as well. No one can truly understand the pain that another person is experiencing. If you claim to understand, there is nothing left to discuss; you already know it all.

It is better to say, "I am sure this must be very painful; tell me how *you* are doing." This line of questioning makes a statement and then asks the mourner for clarification. It opens up the discussion rather than closing it before it begins.

Since the purpose of a Shiva visit is to afford the mourner the opportunity to talk about the deceased, any questions or statements from the visitor should be framed in such a way as to elicit this kind of response. The above are only examples of those types of questions. Be original, be creative, and you will have performed this *mitzvah* in a most meaningful way.

The Post-Shiva Period

Unavoidable as it is, the most difficult period for the mourner is when the formal Shiva period comes to an end. For almost seven days and nights, the mourner is surrounded by loving family and friends. Every one of the mourner's needs is cared for — three meals a day are provided, the house is kept neat and clean, transportation to and from school is arranged for the children, the plants are watered, the dog is walked. Cared for by family, friends and community, the mourner's sole focus was grieving.

As the mourner begins the seventh and final day, however, a change begins to take effect. The mourner is lifted from the low bench upon which she or he has been seated and is walked outside the home, usually accompanied by clergy, family and friends. This act symbolizes the reintroduction of the mourner to the reality of the true world and hints at the necessity of becoming part of it once again.

Now begins the longest and most difficult day in the post-Shiva period. The crowds have gone, the low chairs removed, the furniture rearranged to its original configuration, the mirrors which were covered are exposed, the constant noise and chatter that permeated the room is silenced. For the first time in a week, the mourner is left alone, and may experience a variety of conflicting emotions: perhaps abandonment, perhaps anger, hopefully acceptance; but certainly a deep and indescribable feeling of loneliness.

It is during this period of time of post-Shiva mourning – which has no specific guidelines or time periods – that caring friends and family must be particularly diligent not to abandon the post-Shiva mourner. Despite outward appearances and brave fronts, there is still grief.

The mourner will now begin a new and difficult journey, not one that seeks closure but one that attempts to discover and live with a new reality; one that does not forget the past, but looks to the future with hope, optimism and promise. The emotions of a post-Shiva mourner have been beautifully captured in the following "After Loss Credo," by Barbara Hills

LesStrang, founder of the AfterLoss Grief Recovery
Program:

The After Loss Credo

I need to talk about my loss.

I may often need to tell you what happened —
or to ask you why it happened.

Each time I discuss my loss, I am helping
myself face the reality of the death of my
loved one.

I need to know that you care about me.

I need to feel your touch, your hugs.

I need you just to be "with" me.

(And I need to be with you.)

I need to know you believe in me and in my
ability to get through my grief in my own
way. (And in my own time.)

Please don't judge me now — or think that I'm
behaving strangely.

Remember I'm grieving.

I may even be in shock.

I may feel afraid. I may feel deep rage.

I may even feel guilty. But above all, I hurt.

I'm experiencing a pain unlike any I've ever
felt before.

Don't worry if you think I'm getting better and
  then suddenly I seem to slip backward.
Grief makes me behave this way at times. And
  please don't tell me you "know how I feel,"
  or that it's time for me to get on with my life.
(I am probably already saying this to myself.)
What I need now is time to grieve and to
  recover.
Most of all, thank you for being my friend.
Thank you for your patience.
Thank you for caring.
Thank you for helping, for understanding.
Thank you for praying for me. And remember,
  in the days or years ahead, when you may
  have a loss — when you need me as I have
  needed you — I will understand.
And then I will come and be with you.

Beyond Shiva

My intention in writing this book was to focus primar-
ily on the periods of grief, mourning, the seven day
Shiva following the death of a loved one, and its immediate aftermath. However, there are two other periods
of mourning that also should be noted.

The Sheloshim, *or Thirty-Day Period of Mourning*

The many stringent laws which the mourners are obligated to observe during the seven days of Shiva – such as abstinence from full body bathing and the prohibitions against wearing laundered clothing, shaving, haircuts, wearing leather shoes, and marital relations – are somewhat relaxed during the twenty-three days following the seven days of Shiva. While allowing the mourner to continue grieving at one level, it also reintroduces the mourner to everyday activities.

Just as in the post-Shiva period, the memories of the deceased begin to fade, if ever so slightly, so too must the conditions that keep them alive begin to be somewhat relaxed as well. The transition from sitting Shiva to returning to "normalcy" is difficult. The *Sheloshim* phase recognizes this change and prescribes a way of conduct that allows the mourner additional flexibility in dealing with this new reality. Accordingly, the laws regarding personal conduct and relationships are modified to allow the mourner entrance into this new phase of living.

The Year of Mourning

Every loss is sad. Every loss leaves a deep void which is hard to explain and impossible to fill. Every loss is full of memories that are both joyous and painful to recall. And yet every loss is not the same. Just as during one's life the love one has for a parent, spouse, child, or sibling differs in intensity and manifestation, so too the grief and sadness one experiences upon their death manifests itself differently as well.

Judaism recognizes and respects the special role of parents. We are taught that a child is the product of a collective creation, the culmination of a partnership between man, woman, and God. Although one can have many children or siblings in one's lifetime, and their deaths will undoubtedly cause an immeasurable and profound sense of loss and sadness, still, we only have one set of parents: one mother, one father. Because of this unique and sacred relationship, the mourner's requirement to recite the *Kaddish* prayer is different for parents than for any other family members who have passed away. During the Shiva and the *Sheloshim, Kaddish* is recited for all family members who have passed away. Once the thirty-day period has ended, the mourners are no longer obligated to recite *Kaddish* on a daily basis. The Jewish legal status of mourning has officially ended. The exception is in regard to one's parents. Because of their special connection and relationship to their children, Judaism requires that the "Mourner's *Kaddish*" be recited for eleven months following a parent's death. There are other stringencies that many children take upon themselves as well. Some refrain from all social gatherings, from watching movies, listening to music, or buying new clothing. One's behavior during this time is fairly subjective; when in doubt as to proper observances, one should consult a rabbi who is knowledgeable in this area.

The purpose of proper conduct, whether during the Shiva period, the *Sheloshim*, or the year, is to elevate the soul of the deceased. This can be accomplished in many meaningful ways — through study, introspection, and giving charity to worthwhile causes.

Afterword

My journey with you is coming to an end but hopefully your own journey is just beginning. Each one of us, young and old, will eventually have to face this sequence of events in our lives. Life is a gift that is bestowed upon us from the moment of conception. As we begin to grow in the early years, we naively and inevitably take life for granted. Our youth is filled with activities, involvements, educational opportunities, and romance. Most of us take for granted that we will be blessed with healthy minds and bodies. Illness and sickness are foreign conditions not yet in our vocabularies. The years pass by, slowly at first, and then faster as we reach middle age. We mature; our goals and desires begin to change together with our bodies. We begin to appreciate the blessings of our years, our lives, our families, our relationships, our accomplishments. And then, almost without warning, the "golden years" are upon us and at times the gold begins to fade and requires some corrective "polishing." We are mindful of the years we've attained and begin to concentrate on the years that hopefully remain.

As hinted at in the very beginning of this book, life and death are irrevocably intertwined. Each of us will eventually pass on to another world, another life. If our lives were filled with good deeds towards our fellow man; if our goals and accomplishments were based on the principles of ethical behavior, honesty, and morality; if we have brought joy and happiness to our families and friends; if we've helped those who are less fortunate; if we've made the slightest difference in the life of someone in need — then our lives on this earth will have been purposeful and meaningful.

When we pass to another life, those who mourn us should be comforted in the knowledge that we will be in a better place. Those we leave behind will be able to transition from "Mourning to Morning," secure in the knowledge that we are protected and in God's hands.

May God console all who mourn, together with the mourners of Zion and Jerusalem. And may those who visit the mourners in their time of need be blessed.

Acknowledgments

Among my many supporters there are some in particular who never cease to give me their continued and constant encouragement throughout the long and sometimes arduous hours of writing. I want to express my sincere thankfulness and gratitude to them for having faith in me and for unwittingly giving me the strength and motivation to complete this book.

More than ten years ago, a heavenly rainbow appeared unexpectedly on the horizon and illuminated my darkened skies with its beautiful and colorful hues. Darkness changed to light . . . sadness to joy . . . uncertainty to purposefulness. Though choosing to remain anonymous, this beacon continues to shine brightly for me and brings friendship, caring support, and love that will always be cherished.

A boyhood friend with whom I have just recently re-established a warm relationship has unwittingly helped me to go beyond what I believed were my limited talents. Though we still jokingly argue as to which one of us was the victorious general in our camp color war days, there is no doubt that he has far exceeded anyone's expectations of what he could be in his lifetime. A prolific writer, author of more than thirty books, professor emeritus at Harvard Law School, staunch supporter, defender, and spokesman for the Jewish people and the State of Israel, **Alan (Avi) Dershowitz** has shown me that one can accomplish beyond one's dreams if the effort to do so is properly channeled. Though a second book leaves me far behind Avi's output, at least I've taken a step that I didn't believe possible. Thanks, Avi, for the motivation to attempt and to succeed.

It's been almost twenty years since, by sheer coincidence, a bundle of energy entered my life. Although she is best known for giving advice on other topics, she has always been a source of encouragement and support in any endeavor I've undertaken. Her friendship knows no bounds. **Dr. Ruth Westheimer** continues to inspire me. Her motto, "Don't retire — instead rewire," reinforces my motivation to succeed. Thank you, Dr. Ruth!

I have been privileged to be associated with the Greater Miami Jewish Federation for the past eight years, in particular with Executive Vice President **Rabbi Fredrick Klein**, of its Rabbinic Association. As the creator and driving force behind the establishment of Mishkan Miami, a parachaplaincy program that trains volunteers to visit hospitalized patients and homebound elderly, Fred encouraged me to join its faculty. My lectures to these groups over the past several years have served as the testing grounds for most of the material contained in this book. Thank you, Fred, for your unwavering confidence and support.

I am so fortunate to share my office at Mount Sinai Medical Center with two very special friends: Director of Volunteer Services **Edie Shapiro**, and her most capable assistant, **Jonnie Vargas**. Their friendship and concern for my well-being, their attentiveness to my numerous requests and to the many details that make my efforts successful as the Rabbi/Chaplain of Mount Sinai, are beyond the call of duty. Thank you both for making the workplace so warm and inviting.

Whenever I need a report typed, a manuscript edited, a phrase modified, a concept clarified, there is only one individual I know I can depend upon: **Joelle Silverman Miller**, creator of By Design Communications. She is the consummate professional – not only talented, but honest, reliable, and trustworthy as well. I am so fortunate to have met Joelle almost ten years ago. My gratitude goes to you for all the help and counsel you continue to provide. May you be blessed with good health for many years.

As I noted in my first book, *A Caring Presence*, a symphony orchestra needs a conductor to make certain that the musical composition is performed in the manner the composer intended. **Charlotte Friedland** was that maestro on my "first symphony" and has remained my maestro of choice on my "newest symphony" as well. Her exceptional editing skills in changing a word or substituting a phrase have transformed the many individual sounds into a meaningful composition. Thank you, Charlotte, for all of your help.

Publisher **Tzvi Mauer** immediately expressed his belief that my manuscript would be a valuable contribution to the Jewish community. I am deeply grateful and appreciative to him and his excellent staff at **Urim/ K'tav Publishing** for their efforts and their careful and competent production of this book.

I have been truly blessed by being associated with **Rabbi Dr. Jacob J. Schacter**, the senior scholar at the Center for the Jewish Future at Yeshiva University. Over the years he has been my mentor, my congregational Rabbi, and most of all, my friend. His critical review and analysis of my manuscript has contributed greatly to its readability. Thank you, Rabbi J.J., for all your efforts on my behalf.

I wrote the following in the Acknowledgments section of my first book: "I have always wanted to be an inspiration to my children and grandchildren — to leave them (after 120 years) with some legacy, some accomplishment that they could point to in my life that would add meaning and purpose to their lives as well." There is little that I can add to these previously expressed sentiments. What has increased with the blessing of God is the number of my family members. I still remain so proud of my wonderful and gifted children and their spouses: **Paula** and **Mark Lev; Jacob** and **Edna Schreiber; Miriam** and **Jamie Skydell; David** and **Laurie Schreiber; Nachum** and **Ilene Schwartz.** In addition to being a grandfather to **Joshua, Alex, Jillian; Gavri, Maya, Simi-Tal; Nicole, Andrew, Brian, Jordan; Jeremy, Ami, Aviva** and **Jocelyn,** I have been blessed with three great-grandchildren, **Aaron (AJ), Reese** and **Charlotte.** My cup runneth over!

I would like to express my sincere gratitude and appreciation to my son, **Jacob,** for his guidance and input into this project. Jacob is a gifted, award-winning author and lecturer. His editing and writing skills are outstanding and were invaluable in turning my manuscript into a very readable book. My thanks to you, Jacob, with love.

Writing a book is not an easy task. It requires much time, discipline, and encouragement, particularly when the words seem to dry up and disappear. I am so thankful and fortunate that **Rose**, my wife for thirty-three years, has always remained by my side and believed in me and my creative abilities. Her confidence has given me the motivation to accomplish and succeed — I am truly blessed.

Finally, my heartfelt thanks to God, who has granted me the good fortune of life, strength, health, and contentment. If there is any wisdom to be found in the pages of this book, it is through the grace of God who creates and sustains life and, when death occurs, enables mourners to find solace, comfort, and consolation in their new reality. May we all live to see the day when He will wipe away all of our sorrows and tears and bring only joy and happiness to our lives.

About the Author

RABBI SIMEON SCHREIBER is the founder, director, and lead chaplain of Visiting Chaplain Services, Inc., a not-for-profit agency providing comfort and support to anyone in spiritual or emotional distress. He currently serves as Senior Staff Chaplain at Mount Sinai Medical Center in Miami Beach, Florida, and is the first (ever) chaplain of the Bal Harbour Police Department. He has written and lectured extensively on the guidelines and protocols for those who are sitting Shiva. He is also the author of "A Caring Presence," which contains an in-depth guide to the etiquette of Bikur Cholim visitation.

Rabbi Schreiber is a respected and highly regarded Rabbi and Board Certified Chaplain. He was awarded his Chaplaincy degree from The Health Care Chaplaincy Institute and his board certification from the National Association of Jewish Chaplains. Rabbi Schreiber is a graduate of Yeshiva College and received his rabbinic ordination from the Rabbi Isaac Elchanan Theological Seminary of Yeshiva University. He and his wife, Rose, reside in Bal Harbour, Florida. They have five children and many grandchildren and great-grandchildren.